PYTHONS

BY DON P. ROTHAUS

The Child's World

Published by The Child's World®
1980 Lookout Drive • Mankato, MN 56003-1705
800-599-READ • www.childsworld.com

ACKNOWLEDGMENTS
The Child's World®: Mary Berendes, Publishing Director
Olivia Gregory: Editing
Pamela J. Mitsakos: Photo Research

PHOTO CREDITS
© antoni_halim/iStock.com: 11; bluedogroom/Shutterstock.com: 17;
Derrick Neill/Dreamstime.com: 19; Ecophoto/Dreamstime.com: 7;
e2dan/Shutterstock.com: 8; Ethan Daniels/Shutterstock.com: 5; Gitanna/
Shutterstock.com: 21; Marek Velechovsky/Shutterstock.com: 12;
PhotoDisc: 23; reptiles4all/Shutterstock.com: cover, 1; Susan Flashman/
Shutterstock.com: 15

ISBN 9781631437519
LCCN 2014945445

Printed in the United States of America
Mankato, MN
November, 2014
PA02242

CONTENT ADVISER:
THE ZOOLOGICAL SOCIETY OF SAN DIEGO

ABOUT THE AUTHOR

Don P. Rothaus has a degree in zoology from the University of Washington. He has been a biologist for the state's Department of Fish and Wildlife. His research centers on marine invertebrates, including sea urchins, sea cucumbers, geoduck clams, and abalone. He also enjoys participating in seasonal environmental education and outreach programs for elementary school classrooms in the greater Seattle area. Don is an avid diver and underwater photographer.

TABLE OF CONTENTS

On the cover: Indian pythons like this one live in southern Asia. They are also called black-tailed pythons.

MEET THE PYTHON!

It's thought that most snakes, including pythons, have been around for about 130 million years.

Somewhere in the steamy rain forest, a large snake lies waiting on a tree branch. Nearby, a rat scurries through the brush, unaware of the danger overhead. As the rat busies itself finding food, the snake senses the rat's body warmth. The snake strikes out, wrapping itself tightly around the startled rat. In a few minutes it is over—the rat is dead, and the snake has a meal. The snake swallows the rat whole, then slowly moves away to rest and **digest** its meal. What is this big snake? It's a python!

This Burmese python is coiled on a branch in Myanmar. Burmese pythons live in southern Asia and grow to be about 12 feet (4 m) long.

BIG SNAKES

Pythons and boa constrictors are different animals. Pythons have one more bone in their heads than boas, and they also have a few more teeth. Pythons also lay eggs, while boas give birth to live babies.

Pythons are some of the world's largest snakes. There are 35 different kinds, or **species**, of pythons. The largest is the *Asian reticulated python*, which can grow to be 32 feet (10 m) long and weigh over 300 pounds (136 kg). The smallest species is the *ball python*, which grows to only about 6 feet (2 m) long and weighs about 4 pounds (2 kg).

Each python species shows a different pattern in the coloring of its smooth scales. These patterns allow the snakes to blend in with their surroundings. Scientists call these kinds of protective colors **camouflage**.

You can see the pattern on this southern African rock python. These snakes can be 15 feet (5 m) long. They live in Africa.

SNAKES IN HIDING

Most pythons live in **tropical** rain forests. These areas are full of trees and bushes the snakes can use for camouflage. The tropical rain forests of Africa, Australia, India, Southeast Asia, and the East Indies all are home to pythons. A few python species live in other areas, including dry deserts, high mountains, and grassy plains.

Like all snakes, pythons are **reptiles** that can't make their own body heat. For this reason, wild pythons live only in areas of the world that have warm weather all year long.

Many pythons are excellent swimmers and spend a lot of time in the water.

This African rock python is hiding in some dead leaves.

BELLY WALKERS

Pythons move very slowly—only about 1 mile (1.6 km) an hour.

Pythons don't slither from side to side the way other snakes do. Instead, they move in much the same way as a caterpillar or a centipede. They inch their way forward by moving their belly scales. The scales act like the legs of a caterpillar, helping the animal grip in one spot and pulling it forward in another.

This Burmese python is an albino (al-BY-noh), which means its coloring is much lighter than normal Burmese pythons. Albino animals don't usually live long in the wild because they can't hide very well.

HUNGRY HUNTERS

Pythons are **predators** that feed mostly on small animals and birds. Rodents such as mice and rats are their most common food, or **prey**. Usually pythons eat one small animal in a meal. They have several such meals every week. But sometimes, a hungry python will kill a larger animal. In fact, large pythons are able to eat animals weighing 100 pounds (45 kg)! If a python does eat a big meal, it won't eat again for several weeks—or even months.

Humans are much too large and quick to be common prey for pythons. Although python attacks on humans do occur, they are very rare. A person faces a much greater chance of being hit by lightning than of being attacked by a python!

Pythons can only eat in warm weather. If the weather is too cold (below about 50°F, or 10°C), pythons won't eat at all.

This ball python is eating a mouse. Ball pythons (also called royal pythons) only grow to be about 6 feet (2 m) long. They are sometimes kept as pets.

FINDING FOOD

Green tree pythons have been known to use the tips of their tails as lures. When the snake wiggles its tail, mice and birds think it's a worm or other tasty treat and move in for a closer look.

Like other snakes, pythons have small pits near the sides of their mouths. These pits help pythons sense their prey's body heat so they can aim and strike successfully—even if it's too dark out to see.

Spotted pythons have been known to wait at cave entrances to catch bats that fly out each night.

Unlike some snakes, pythons don't use **venom** to kill their prey. Instead, they capture their prey by hiding in trees or brush and surprising animals that stray too near. They use their sense of smell to decide whether the animal would make a good meal. The snake's tongue flicks in and out quickly, bringing with it the scent of the surrounding air. In the roof of its mouth, the snake has a small scent organ, called a *Jacobson's organ*, that is far more sensitive than the human nose.

Once the snake decides to attack, it finds its prey by sensing the other animal's body heat. The snake lunges forward and grasps its prey by the head. Then it coils tightly around its victim and squeezes tighter every time the captured animal breathes out. This squeezing process is called **constriction**. Finally, the prey is unable to breathe and dies. The python must be very powerful to kill its prey in this way.

A python can swallow animals larger than its own head! Instead of the long fangs found in venomous snakes, pythons have many small, sharp teeth. The teeth hold the food tightly while the snake unlocks its jaw and stretches its mouth.

The python then tightens muscles that draw the prey farther and farther down the snake's throat and into its stomach. After the snake swallows a large animal, it has a lump you can see! The lump moves slowly through the snake's **digestive system** and toward its tail.

This scrub python is eating a baby bird. Scrub pythons live in Indonesia, Papua New Guinea, and Australia.

Many people wonder how a python can breathe with its mouth full of food. It has a special tube in the bottom of its mouth that stays open when it eats, allowing the snake to breathe.

PYTHON BABIES

Depending on the species, python mothers lay 2 to 80 eggs.

Sometimes python mothers look as if they are hiccupping or shivering as they cover and protect their eggs in colder weather. These are really small muscle movements that keep the eggs a little warmer.

Pythons mate in the spring, and the female lays her eggs in the early summer. She coils her body around her **clutch** of eggs to keep them warm and safe. The sun also helps to warm the eggs while the babies develop inside. The mother stays with the eggs day and night for two months.

Finally, the eggs are ready to hatch. Each baby python uses a small, sharp spine called an **egg tooth** to tear a hole in its egg. From this point on, the baby is on its own, learning to catch food and defend itself against other predators. A baby reticulated python might be 20 to 26 inches (51 to 66 cm) long when it hatches and weigh only 4 ounces (113 g).

This baby ball python is hatching out of its egg. Snake eggs aren't hard like birds' eggs. Instead, they're soft and leathery. They tear and rip rather than breaking.

GROWING

The heaviest living snake is a Burmese python named Baby. She weighs 403 pounds (183 kg) and lives at the Serpent Safari Park in Gurnee, Illinois.

The longest python ever recorded—a reticulated python—was 32 feet, 9.5 inches (10 m) long.

As you grow, your skin grows with you. But a snake's skin is different—it stays the same size, even as the snake grows larger. When a python gets too big for its skin, it rubs against trees and rocks. The old, dry skin soon comes off, revealing a new one waiting underneath. This process of losing the old skin is called **shedding**.

Pythons continue to grow throughout their entire lives. How fast they grow depends on how well they do at capturing food. During its first year, a young python might grow to three times its original length. Pythons grow more slowly as they get older, but they never really stop. Large snakes like pythons can live for 20 or 30 years!

You can see the old skin that this green tree python has just shed. These pythons live in New Guinea, Indonesia, and parts of Australia.

IMPORTANT SNAKES

Woma pythons usually hunt animals that live in burrows— where there isn't much room for the snakes to coil around their prey. Instead, these pythons squash their prey against the burrow wall until the victim runs out of air.

Many people fear pythons and other snakes, but these animals play an important role in nature. Every year pythons eat countless rodents such as mice and rats, keeping the numbers of these animals down. Rodents damage crops and spread diseases. Without enemies such as pythons and other snakes, the number of rodents would soar, causing heavy damage and disease. By understanding these giant snakes and the important role they play, perhaps people can replace their fear with respect.

Big Burmese pythons like this one can weigh up to 200 pounds (91 kg).

GLOSSARY

camouflage (KAM-oo-flazh) Camouflage is special coloring or markings that help an animal blend in with its surroundings. All pythons have camouflage.

clutch (KLUTCH) A clutch is a group of eggs. Python clutches have 2 to 80 eggs.

constriction (kon-STRIK-shun) Constriction is tight squeezing. Pythons use constriction to kill their prey.

digest (DY-jest) To digest food is to break it down in one's stomach. Pythons need warm areas in order to digest their food.

digestive system (dy-JEST-iv SIS-tem) The digestive system of an animal includes the organs it uses to break down food. A python's digestive system includes its stomach and intestines.

egg tooth (EGG TOOTH) An egg tooth is a hard bump that some baby animals develop on their noses as they grow inside their eggs. When it is time to hatch, the baby use its egg tooth to break through the surface of the egg.

predators (PRED-uh-terz) Predators are animals that hunt and eat other animals. Pythons are predators.

prey (PRAY) Prey are animals that are eaten as food. Mice and rats are the most common prey for pythons.

reptiles (REP-tylz) Reptiles are animals that have backbones, lungs, and tough skin covered with scales. Reptiles need outside heat to warm their bodies. Pythons are reptiles.

shedding (SHED-ding) Shedding is losing an older skin. Pythons shed as they grow.

species (SPEE-sheez) An animal species is a group of animals that share the same features and can have babies only with animals in the same group. There are 35 different python species.

tropical (TROP-ik-ull) Tropical areas are those that have warm, moist weather all year long.

venom (VEN-um) Venom is a type of poison that some snakes produce. Pythons do not have venom.

TO FIND OUT MORE

Watch It!

Ball Pythons in the Wild. DVD. Pottsville, PA: Cottrello Associates, 2005.

Read It!

Cannon, Janell. *Verdi*. San Diego: Harcourt Brace, 1997.

Cheng, Christopher. *Python*. Somerville, MA: Candlewick Press, 2013.

Ethan, Eric. *Boas, Pythons, and Anacondas*. Milwaukee, WI: Gareth Stevens, 1995.

Sexton, Colleen. *Pythons*. Minneapolis, MN: Bellwether Media, 2010.

Weber, Valerie J. *Reticulated Pythons.* Milwaukee, WI: Gareth Stevens, 2003.

Wechsler, Doug. *Pythons*. New York: Rosen, 2001.

On the Web

Visit our home page for lots of links about pythons:
www.childsworld.com/links

Note to Parents, Teachers, and Librarians: We routinely check our Web links to make sure they're safe, active sites—so encourage your readers to check them out!

INDEX

DATE DUE

			PRINTED IN U.S.A.